to Jack Henry !

Rusty

The Story of One Lucky Dog

Who lived Sun Valley!

Sophie & Derek Craighead
Illustrated by Maxton Beckwith

Maxton B

Sophie
August
2012

Derek Craighead

For information about permission to reproduce
selections from this book, write to:
MQD Press PO Box 50703 Santa Barbara, CA 93150

Printed in the United States of America

Craighead, Sophie.
Rusty: the story of one lucky dog/ Sophie & Derek
Craighead; illustrated by Maxton Beckwith.
p. cm.
SUMMARY: A golden retriever mix lives a tough life
chained to a tire until he is rescued by two caring
neighbors and adopted by a wonderful family. With his
new family he plays in rivers, jumps in lakes and even
goes for airplane rides.
Library of Congress Control Number 2012941715
ISBN 978-0-615-65500-0

1. Golden retriever--Juvenile fiction. 2. Families--
Juvenile fiction. [1. Golden retriever--Fiction.
2. Dogs--Fiction. 3. Family life--Fiction.]
I. Craighead, Derek. II. Beckwith, Maxton, ill.
III. Title

PZ7.C8444Rus 2012

MQD Press
TM

For Scotty and Sage ~ S.C. & D.C.

For Brooke and Blake ~ M.B.

As far back as Rusty could remember, each day started and ended chained to a discarded trailer. Sleeping behind an old truck tire, Rusty only dreamed he could run through the fields with his brother. Sneezing the dust from his nose, Rusty breathed in the morning dampness and the smell of fresh cut hay.

In view, but out of reach of Rusty, Lucky's short chain anchored him to an old boat. As the sun rose, each dog had to dig into the dry and dusty ground for shade.

The rumble of their owner's engine reached Rusty and Lucky even before they saw the old red pickup truck. Not knowing what to expect, Rusty hunkered down and softly patted his tail on the hard packed earth. He wanted to take his owner, and Lucky, for a wild romp across the road and into the shrubs and tall grass, but the man just went into the trailer and slammed the door.

When the kitchen lights were finally turned off for the evening, Rusty and Lucky could tell that it would be yet another night with no food.

As the evening air carried the excited barks and yips of several coyotes hunting their dinner in the hay field, Rusty could not help himself- and he cried out in frustration.

His howl was returned by a yap from a lone coyote on a nearby peak. The coyote sounded so happy and free from its lofty perch. For a moment, both dogs felt this coyote's freedom, and Lucky chimed in with an even louder outcry. This only brought angry yells from the man inside the house. Rusty and Lucky circled round on their chains, curling into golden brown balls; their damp, black noses tucked into the warmth of their tails.

Each night at bedtime, there were interesting and curious things to think about. And deep down, Rusty always knew that there would be a better life for him and his brother. Rusty happily thought about this every night after the lights went out.

The two Golden Retrievers fell asleep dreaming, not of their scolding, nor of the cold and hunger, but of the morning's warm sun, and the meadowlark's song.

As the days grew shorter and colder, two alert neighbors named Ron and Mary Ann began to notice Rusty and Lucky's baleful howls. They had also noticed that the dogs were never let off their chains, and never seemed to have enough food. In fact, Ron and Mary Ann had for some time believed the dogs were being mistreated. From the road, they could see how skinny the dogs were, and how their constricting collars were growing tighter around their necks.

After much talk about what would be best for the dogs, Ron and Mary Ann offered to buy Lucky and Rusty from the owner. After days of negotiating, Rusty and Lucky were purchased for $50.00.

Finally freed from his chain, Rusty bolted to Lucky. The two whined and wrapped their front legs around each other's necks, and licked each other's noses. The dog-hug turned into a playful wrestling match, and then when Lucky was unchained, a run amok chase of bump and bite. Now full of high spirits, the two dogs jumped into the neighbor's car.

Ron and Mary Ann soon found a home that wanted to adopt BOTH Rusty and Lucky. What a miracle this was!

In their new home, the two dogs soaked up all the newfound attention and love, and had NO problem eating two meals a day!

They slowly recovered and began to relax in their cozy new home. Never having been inside a house, there was much to discover.

It was a whole new world, and not without challenges. In the beginning both dogs were scared by the television, and the first few trips down the stairs gave Rusty quite a tumble!

Rusty and Lucky quickly discovered how truly fun life could be! Each day was now a new adventure.

From playing with the geese in the gentle pools of the Gros Ventre River...

... to boating on nearby lakes.

These two dogs were definitely happy to explore all of this new land under the majestic granite peaks of the Teton Range.

Rusty and Lucky even got to go for airplane rides!

They traveled far to the north, and rode in canoes down clear, Canadian rivers, as their owners fished for Atlantic Salmon.

Rusty and Lucky were now living a life that they had only ever imagined.

Rusty and Lucky truly loved each one of these incredible adventures, but most of all, they loved returning to their wonderful home nestled beneath the Teton Mountains.

THE END

Rusty, The Story of One Lucky Dog is a true story about the real life rescue of two Golden Retriever mixes. These dogs were found by Ron and Mary Ann Ahrens and adopted by Sophie, Derek, Scotty and Sage Craighead. Rusty and Lucky immediately became part of the Craighead family, which at the time of the new dogs' arrival included Billy (the Amazon Parrot), Eddie Big Beak (a pet Raven), Ruby (a Newfoundland), Tessie (an English Setter), Dipper (a Golden Retriever), and Roger (another Golden)!

In gratitude for the tremendous pet rescues of Ron and Mary Ann Ahrens, the Craigheads helped build Lucky's Place, the Star Valley Animal Shelter. A portion of the proceeds from this book benefits Lucky's Place and other no kill animal shelters.

In memory of Jean Craighead George...
author, naturalist and inspiration to generations.

Photo © 2012 ~ Lucy Brown

Sophie Craighead, with Lucky, Dipper (front) and Rusty